CLIVE BARKER: MYTHMAK

CLIVE BARKER

MYTHMAKER FOR THE MILLENNIUM

SUZANNE J. BARBIERI

First published in Great Britain in 1994 by

The British Fantasy Society
2 Harwood Street
Stockport SK4 1JJ

Cover illustration © 1994 Les Edwards
Internal illustrations © 1994 Pete Queally
Layout and design by Michael Marshall Smith
Publication co-ordinated by David J. Howe
for the British Fantasy Society

ISBN 0 952 4153 0 5
BFS 001

British Library Cataloguing in Publication Data.
A catalogue record for this book is available
from the British Library.

Printed and bound in Great Britain by
The Longdunn Press Limited,
Barton Manor, St Philips, Bristol BS2 0RL.

ACKNOWLEDGMENTS

Thanks to:

The BFS for taking the plunge; Big G and the Seven; Les Edwards; Val Paine; Mike Marshall Smith; Pete Queally; Chris Kenworthy; Kevin Rivers; Kate Farquhar-Thomson; Rosemary Howe; Debbie Bennett; Stephen Payne; Peter Atkins for eleventh hour miracles; my Mum for a magical upbringing; My husband Richard for everything and more; Clive Barker, and most importantly, David J Howe (without whom this book would not be what it is) for focus, support, tireless enthusiasm and wondrous deeds too numerous to mention.

This book is dedicated to everyone who worked on it, had a hand in it, inspired it and encouraged it, and to everyone who matters to me. You all know who you are.

SJB August 1994

contents

foreword

The publication of *Clive Barker: Mythmaker for the Millennium* is something I welcome for many reasons. We'll come on to those that relate specifically to its subject in a moment. For me, though, the very existence of this book is cause for celebration because it marks the initial venture into a wider publishing world by The British Fantasy Society.

For more than two decades the BFS has done sterling service to 'fantasy', that strange catch-all genre to which so many of us turn for entertainment and illumination in whatever metaphorical shapes our tastes demand – spaceships, demons, or corvette-driving elves. But that service has been done essentially in secret – booklets, conventions and newsletters, all in the main known only to its membership. Now, having shaken off its fetching shyness, the BFS is announcing itself to the general public. Please support its immodesty and enthusiasm. In other words – stop reading this on the train-station bookstall and buy it.

Now. Clive Barker. Well, what a long strange road it's been. And how quickly (and increasingly quickly) the years pass. The difference between chronological time and perceived time is worthy of an essay (or a novel) in itself but I don't have the (perceived) time to write it. What I can say, though, is that it seems like a couple of years – and is actually twenty – since Clive and I used to sign on together for our dole cheques at Renshaw Hall in Liverpool.

Was he different, then? Well, he was certainly poorer. And so was the world of imaginative literature – for Clive was yet to write any of the works that have inspired the intelligent and critically acute essay by Suzanne Barbieri that you are about to read. What an interesting, however, are the ways in which he was not different at all. While the state was busy providing me, Clive, and our colleagues (most notably Doug Bradley, the actor who went on to play Pinhead in the *Hellraiser* movies) with unofficial artistic subsidies (i.e. the giro), we were busy crafting theatre-pieces that played in tiny no-budget venues around the country and that centred around precisely the type of concerns that Ms Barbieri takes such delight in finding within the pages of Clive's fiction: Jungian archetypes; mythic structures; the interfaces of Eros and Thanatos; the rage of the phallo-theocracies; and all kinds of other interesting goodies.

The consistency of intent in all of Clive's work from 1974 to 1994 is striking. In a field dominated too often in our day by authors whose sound and fury fill hundreds of pages while still signifying nothing, even critics hostile to his work would have to acknowledge this about Clive – at least he has a point of view. His books are about something. And some of those things they are about will be illuminated for you as soon as I bugger off and let you turn the page to begin reading Ms Barbieri's thought-provoking essay.

Peter Atkins
Hellraiser scriptwriter
Los Angeles
July 1994

MAN
MYTH, AND
MAGIC

"All our joys are but fantastical."

JOHN DONNE

As children we are fed a steady stream of magic in the form of fairy tales and myths. We are led into enchanted forests to do battle with dragons, and to join in fairy revels.

Then when we grow up, our imaginations fuelled and eager to expand, the rug is snatched from under us, and we are told we are too old to believe such stories, and that we must weigh ourselves down with the concerns of the real world; magic doesn't exist, and dreams are to be dismissed as fancy.

But much of our early experience of the complexities of the vital inner world, the psyche, is gained through contact with fairy tales, myths and dreams, which describe all permutations of human experience in the universal language of symbols and archetypes: the language of the Collective Unconscious.

Some, however, never quite 'grow up', and turn to the genres of Horror and Fantasy to satisfy the need to experience this hidden side.

Man has always been hungry for stories. From the lullaby tales that induce infant slumber, to the camp-fire terrors that keep sleep at bay, the promise of losing oneself in some other world is irresistible. Irresistible because we already know that world.

Mankind walks between two worlds: the mundane conscious world of physical being, and a richer subconscious world of dreams and symbols. Something is needed to help maintain this balancing act; so fantastic fiction becomes a means of understanding the two very different sides.

But not all fiction sheds light where it is perhaps most needed.

Before discovering the work of Clive Barker I was becoming disillusioned with the genres of Horror and Fantasy. The books and films seemed jaded and formulaic; simple rehashes of already tired plots.

Then someone gave me a copy of *Weaveworld*.

At last I had found what I had been wanting: here was magic, here was terror, here was love and madness, dreams and nightmares; and more importantly, here was something that touched deeper than any fiction could: here was the stuff of myth.

The point at which fiction becomes fable, story becomes myth is when the theme has a power beyond the actual storyline, and the characters represent archetypes that speak to us in a more direct way than their apparent personalities and actions do, pulling together the whole like a prophetic dream whose meaning is greater than the sum of its images.

The genres of Horror and Fantasy have often been wrongly labelled escapist. Perhaps this is true at the lower end of the scale, but imaginative fiction at its best is confrontational at the deepest level; for it is only by grappling with our fears and bringing the darker aspects of ourselves out in the open that we can learn to understand and integrate them.

Barker's work does just that. It recognises that the devil is as much a part of our nature as the angel, and that to deny that devil a voice is to light a slow burning fuse that will eventually blow up in your face.

By approaching his work in a mythological way, by using archetypes whose very natures reinforce their message, Barker's stories reach the parts that mere fiction cannot touch, thereby offering a valuable insight into the human and inhuman condition.

True mythology must represent the spirit of the age if it is to remain relevant. For the past two thousand years we have been living in the astrological Age of Pisces, whose symbol is two fishes swimming in opposite directions. This symbol represents the split between opposites; the duality of Man and his Shadow, mind and matter, flesh and spirit. The Piscean Age is also the Age of the one God; and of logical masculine thought.

With the advent of the millennium, we will move into the Age of Aquarius: an Age of unity of opposites, integration of Conscious and Unconscious. This is a time when dreams bleed into waking life, and thought is made solid: an Age of feminine feeling and the re-emergence of the Goddesses.

Therefore, as we move into the Aquarian Age, we must bring with us a mythology that is in line with the needs of that age. Who better to supply that new mythology than Clive Barker?

With tales of androgynes, shape shifters, hidden worlds and flesh remade by act of will, Barker's work is ideally suited to this ethos of blurring the boundaries between dreams and reality.

Within these pages we explore the parallels between five of Barker's other worlds and the progress of the soul from death and rebirth through experience of the conscious, the unconscious, the collective unconscious and the super conscious.

We also look at some of Barker's female characters and establish how their peculiar powers earn them a place in the mythology of the Goddess influenced New Age.

Everyone will place their own interpretations on Clive Barker's work according to their tastes, expectations, and personal belief system. My own views are coloured by my interest in the occult, Tarot in particular; dreams, myths and the work of C.G.Jung.

Of those who are already familiar with Barker's work, not everyone will agree with the interpretations I have attached to its symbolism, nor should they, as imaginative fiction at its multi-layered best should be all things to all people.

part one

other worlds/inner space

"

So
many
worlds,
so much
to do.

"

ALFRED LORD TENNYSON

other worlds, inner space

The Quintessential Worlds of Clive Barker.

Man has always had a fatal yearning for that 'other place', be it Paradise, Neverland or our own dreamworld, everyone longs for the world where magic is commonplace, women are winged and little boys never grow up.

Among the tales of Avalon and Atlantis room must be made for the Imajica, Quiddity, the Fugue, Midian, and the puzzlebox Hell of the Cenobites.

The worlds Clive Barker creates take us deep into the uncharted territory of the psyche. While his worlds are every bit as magical as Narnia and Wonderland, they have a darkness at heart that holds a thin veil between Heaven and Hell. For nothing can exist without its opposite, and the nature of Paradise cannot be understood without a Purgatory with which to compare it.

These five of Barker's worlds can be seen to chart the progress of a soul's journey to completeness through experiencing and understanding the different components of the psyche, and through integrating the conscious beliefs and the hidden knowledge of the unconscious. The term 'Individuation' was coined by Jung to describe this ongoing process of the search for the higher Self.

Within each of these worlds we explore a different part of the inner self, and are confronted by various aspects of the psyche in the guise of archetypal characters and situations. Some of the stories are epiphanies, revealing wonders; others are more cautionary tales. We begin with a visit to the coldest, darkest reaches of the inner self ...

THE HELLBOUND HEART

DEATH OF EGO, BIRTH OF THE SHADOW

The novella that spawned the film *Hellraiser* marries the themes of *Pandora's Box* and *Doctor Faustus*.

Frank Cotton is the ultimate egoist; a waster with an unquenchable hunger for sensation, he sees everything in terms of his own gratification. Frank is the Faustian central character who will go to any lengths for experience.

Frank purchases Lemarchand's configuration, a puzzlebox promised to conceal wonders; but a box represents a coffin, and therefore death, and Frank cannot be transformed without first experiencing the death of his old self.

Frank works at the box for hours. There seems to be no way into it, no hint on its smooth sides of a solution to the riddle. It is quite by accident that his fingers find the pressure points that disengage one section of the box from another and lead him into a world of sights, sensations and exquisite agony, presided over by the Cenobites.

But every dream has its nightmare, and no one has a ruder awakening to this than Frank. When he summons the Cenobites with offerings of petals and doves' heads, he is expecting them to come bearing gifts of perfumed women, hungry for him. Instead all he gets are the Cenobites themselves; corpse-cold, scarred and flagellant:

"A fitful phosphorescence came with them, like the glow of deep-sea fishes: blue, cold; charmless ... he saw nothing of joy, or even humanity, in their maimed faces."

And the pleasures they offer are of a wholly different kind to what Frank has been expecting.

Frank's senses are heightened to such a degree that the slightest odour is sickening, every sight and sound a devastating revelation, and the reel of memories that unspool inside his head more than enough to render him helpless. And just as he thinks it is all over, the trip begins in earnest with the unveiling of the fourth Cenobite, a Kali-esque figure who:

"... sat on a pile of rotting human heads ... their tongues – twenty or more – laid out in ranks on her oiled thighs ... She stood up. The tongues fell to the floor, like a rain of slugs.

"'Now we can begin,' she said."

Frank's physical body is destroyed, but his spirit remains in the room until, awakened by the blood of his brother Rory, his Shadow (the dark, uncivilised side of a person) emerges, twisted and skinless.

Frank has shed his skin, and with it his facade of humanity. He is now a dark primaeval creature whose primary motivation is his own survival, and for this he must have blood.

The sustenance he requires is brought to him by his brother's wife Julia. Driven by her obsessive desire for Frank, she lures men back to the house and murders them so that he may use their blood to grow himself a new skin.

Frank thinks he has outwitted the Cenobites, but he sold his soul in return for experience, and must keep his side of the bargain. Like Doctor Faustus, Frank has entered a Hell of his own making, and the Cenobites, once freed, can never be truly banished. The puzzlebox is only a rudimentary jail whose locks can be easily picked.

The experiences offered by the puzzlebox Hell are of the Unconscious and Frank's mistake is in trying to allow his Shadow self to exist in the physical world. He has been transformed that he may experience the dark dream world, and there is no turning back.

Finally when he is tricked, like Rumpelstiltskin, into saying his own name, the Cenobites home in on him and return to take him back to where he now belongs.

The Hellbound Heart represents the first stage of the individuation process. The old self dies, the outmoded ideals are shed, and the Shadow is dragged raw and kicking into the world of inner experience.

That Frank's Shadow is skinless illustrates the vulnerability of the untutored primal soul, and emphasises that the journey to completeness will be far from painless.

Experience is the best teacher, and the first lesson is that there is no gain without sacrifice.

WAKING THE WEAVE

UNCONSCIOUS BECOMING CONSCIOUS.

Weaveworld, an archetypal fairytale, is about the birth of worlds, and a tribe cast out of Eden, the Seerkind. As Barker himself writes:

"It was the end of the world, and the beginning of worlds."

The Seerkind are a tribe in hiding, and the Fugue, their home, is a patchwork Faeryland woven into a carpet. A carpet was chosen as the best means of disguise, because, as one of the Seerkind says: "What's more easily overlooked than the thing you're standing on?"

Thus the Fugue is relegated to the realm of the Unconscious. However, it is eager to wake into Consciousness, and reveals hints of its hidden riches. Having been asleep for almost a century, the knots are restless; the Gyre at its centre attracts every bird in the area to congregate and trace its spiral.

Cal Mooney, in pursuit of a lost bird, climbs onto a garden wall in an attempt to coax down his errant racing pigeon. In the yard below lays the carpet. Cal reaches for the bird, his foot slips and he falls from the wall.

In the moments before he hits the ground Cal glimpses the carpet's secret. As his eyes scan its intricate design, the knots seem to shift: warp and weft grow into landscapes, coloured threads become grass and sky and the carpet's central medallion design gives way to a constantly spiralling cloud mass, the Gyre. All too quickly the Fugue hides itself again leaving him to land painfully on a worn carpet.

After Cal's first glimpse of the Fugue he knows that his life has been irrevocably changed. At last he has found the place he has been yearning for since childhood, a land of "... miracles, all mystery, all blue shadow and sweet-breathed spirits."

Cal is a dreamer on the verge of waking. His inner self knows there is magic in the world, but his conscious mind is not yet ready to admit it. His first sight of the world within the carpet is, in effect, his first flash of insight.

The unconscious image, the dream message, bursts through into the physical world for a moment, then draws back into itself before it can be analysed, but it leaves its legacy in the form of the knowledge, albeit uncertain, that wonders exist, and that life is worth living if only in the hope that some such glimpse may be had again.

Cal is not content to leave it at that. Having hooked a mystery only to have it slip away, he goes all out to reel it in. His first port of call is the house on Rue Street in whose yard the carpet was laid. The carpet has gone but Cal finds instead an ally in Suzanna Parrish whose Grandmother is the Fugue's last custodian.

Suzanna provides the link between Cal and the Fugue, the Conscious and the Unconscious. She has Seerkind blood along with access to the menstruum, a rare and powerful magic possessed only by women.

Before meeting Suzanna, Cal is lacking a female element in his life. He lives with his widowed father, and although he has a girlfriend, Geraldine, he has no real emotional commitment to her.

In some respects Suzanna is Cal's Anima, the unconscious feminine element in every male. His first sight of the Fugue is in her Grandmother's back yard, and it is only through her that he is able to enter it. Suzanna guides and protects him throughout the story, healing him when he is injured, caring for him when he falls into a fugue state himself.

Yet Suzanna is also one of the most powerful characters in the story. It is she, the wise feminine Unconscious, who is the waker and remaker of worlds.

The ease and practicality with which Suzanna carries on her everyday life whilst acting as custodian of the Fugue is opposed by Cal's difficulty in handling the changes that have taken place in his life.

Cal's obsessive nature is apparent from the start. Since childhood he has made a point of memorising facts, and even now has total recall of the timetable of the trains in and out of his native Liverpool. His own imagination is almost too much for him; he dwells in it at the expense of his physical well-being.

His confrontation with a creature that believes itself to be the Angel Uriel proves too much for Cal's fragile mind and leaves him almost comatose. He falls into a dreamy shadowland where he is dust in the wilderness.

Cal lives in a trance, unable to communicate in any way. No one can help him but himself. He is lost until a chance sighting of his own reflection in a night blackened window reminds him who he is and of his place in the Fugue.

Through finding his Self, Cal is able to heal his fractured psyche. By bringing the Fugue out of hiding and into the physical world, Cal re-establishes contact with his unconscious and unites it with his conscious, thus enabling his mind to function fully again.

MIDIAN

DOWN INTO THE UNCONSCIOUS

The novel *Cabal* concerns the personality; the face we show to the world at large as opposed to our true hidden selves. The story examines the concepts of Duality and Persona, and the discovery of the Unconscious.

The legendary underground city of Midian is home to the Tribes of the Moon; the Nightbreed.

Despite the appearances of the Breed, and their taste for human flesh, they are not the villains. The real monsters are the humans who have for centuries persecuted the Breed for the crime of being different.

The story's main character, Aaron Boone, makes the journey down into Midian and discovers the truth about duality, his own included.

Many of the Breed are literally 'two-faced'. When moving in the outside world, the Conscious, they wear human faces, while in Midian, the Unconscious, they wear their beast-faces; their true faces. As does everyone. None more so than Boone's psychiatrist Dr Decker.

Decker's alter-ego is a serial killer called the Mask. 'Persona' (the term coined by Jung to describe the public face behind which we conceal our true self), is the Latin word for an actor's mask.

Decker frames Boone for the murders he has committed as the Mask. Boone, plagued for much of his life with mental problems, has put his trust in Dr Decker, and although he cannot remember ever having committed the murders, he feels he shouldn't doubt the doctor's words.

Boone first hears whispers of Midian whilst in an asylum. Midian, they say, is a place of refuge for those with nothing left to cling to; the monsters and outcasts of society whose last hope is of finding the one place that will take them in and forgive them their sins however profane those sins might be.

Boone has reached the lowest point of his life. He believes himself to be a murderer, and is on the run. After a failed suicide attempt he decides that if death cannot embrace him, his place is in Midian.

After travelling many miles across virtually desolate terrains Midian appears as if out of nowhere. Boone's first explorations of Midian would have it a ghost town. Lightless and empty, it appears to be uninhabited. Desolate, he heads off to the town's vast cemetery in search of a place to rest his weary body.

As he sleeps Midian stirs, as though from the depths of his dreams. At first an animal's growls invade his dreams, waking him; then from the shadows, two creatures emerge who challenge his right to enter their refuge. One of these creatures is the shape-shifting Peloquin "... more reptile than mammal" who transforms before Boone's eyes, inhaling his lizard features like cigarette smoke. Boone's pleas that he belongs in Midian are ridiculed by Peloquin who insists that Boone is not the murderer he thinks he is: "You're not Nightbreed ...You're meat ... meat for the beast."

Thus Boone is at first denied Midian, because he is not ready. It takes death to make him ready. He must cast off his old life and outmoded concepts of reality so that he may be reborn into the richer world of the Unconscious. Only then may he enter the underground city of Midian.

Yet Boone's literal and symbolic death is a willing sacrifice. He wants so much to explore his Unconscious and understand his duality that no price is too much.

What Boone discovers is that he does indeed have a secret self, and that other self is not a murderer, but the Saviour of the Breed, he is Cabal, "who unmade Midian", and who will remake it in the image of his choosing.

Unlike Decker, whose suppressed dark side takes him over, Boone accepts his duality and takes on board the lessons of the Unconscious, and is made whole by the knowledge that he is something more and other than human.

QUIDDITY

THE ART OF DREAMS AND SHAMEN

Evolution through The Collective Unconscious.

"Memory, prophesy and fantasy — the past, the future and the dreaming moment between them — are all one country, living one immortal day. To know that is wisdom. To use it is the Art."
('The Great and Secret Show')

Between the Cosm and the Metacosm is Quiddity. The Cosm is our world and the Metacosm is the world inhabited by the Iad Uroboros, a nightmare species who form and are formed by the darkest fears of humanity. Quiddity, the dream-sea, is the source of all dreams, all magic, and therefore the Collective Unconscious.

Every person gets just three dips in Quiddity: the first during the first night's sleep outside the womb, the second the night you sleep beside the love of your life, and the third on the last night of your life. Any more than three visits and, says the shaman Kissoon, "We wouldn't be human." The Art is Quiddity's lock and key against those who would seek to control it, for "Quiddity must be preserved, at any cost".

The Great and Secret Show, the first book of the Art, begins with everything in equal balance. For every positive there is a negative: Fletcher, the being of light, is opposed by the Jaff who stands for darkness; and the Jaff's children, the McGuire twins, are equal opposites; similarly beautiful, but Tommy-Ray taking after his evil father and Jo-Beth the epitome of goodness. The two writers who are thrust into the main frame of the action, journalist Nathan Grillo, and screenwriter Tesla Bombeck, are old friends but very different in personality.

The Great and Secret Show is heavy with fourfold symbolism: the four Virgins: Joyce McGuire, Arleen Farrell, Trudi Katz and Carolyn Hotchkiss; the four shamans: Kissoon, The Jaff, Fletcher and Tesla; and the four villages of Palomo Grove: Laureltree, Stillbrook, Windbluff and Deerdell.

The number four has long represented the world of matter. It indicates logic, reason and will-power. The fourfold division occurs frequently in esoteric, mythological and religious symbolism, for example:-

The Four Worlds of the Qabalists: Origination, Creation, Formation and Action; the four beasts of the Apocalypse and of Ezekiel's vision: Lion, Man, Eagle and Bull; Jung's four personality types: Intuition, Feeling, Thinking and Sensation; the four suits of the Tarot: Wands, Cups, Swords and Pentacles, and the corresponding elements of Fire, Water, Air and Earth.

The town of Palomo Grove itself represents stability taken too far. The residents are so devoid of imagination, that when Fletcher draws out their fantasies to build his troops of 'hallucigenia', the best they can come up with are the characters from television soap operas.

Yet little by little, this balance breaks down. The inhabitants of the Grove keep sordid secrets behind the facade of perfection; the cracks they have papered over (in the town as well as their lives, as the ground beneath the Grove is riddled with faults) begin to show.

The stability of the fourfold world is thrown into confusion, and the ultimate balance, that between the dream world and the waking world is threatened when the Jaff creates the schism and opens the way to Quiddity.

The Great and Secret Show is essentially a tale of evolution. No one escapes untouched, but the emphasis is on enhancement rather than simple change: thus the great become greater, the ape becomes human and the flesh becomes spirit. However, it also follows that evil is magnified, and ugly thoughts shape the flesh to suit the sentiment.

Randolph Jaffe, spurred by his desire to control the world's dream life, changes from a tired of life no-hoper to a powerful shaman enhanced by the nuncio, a substance that causes physical and mental evolution; and finally, afraid of his power and burnt out by it, is reduced to almost a shell.

Richard Wesley Fletcher, physically weak and blind in one eye from staring at the sun, becomes a being of light. His penultimate act is to pass the baton of his mission to Tesla before going out in a blaze of glory, his spirit touching each and every one of the Grovers and changing them also.

Fletcher's laboratory ape, Raul becomes a man, and then his spirit becomes part of Tesla, who undergoes the greatest transformation of all, becoming first a shaman, then the long-awaited Saviour.

Like that of Quiddity, the experience of the collective unconscious is one both evolutionary and revelatory. Once it is understood that the imagery of dreams and myths is one common to us all, we can begin to uncover the wisdom within us, and thus begin our spiritual evolution.

IMAJICA

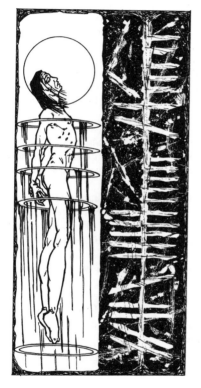

THE CIRCLE CLOSES

Reconciliation with the Higher Self.

"Thus men forgot that all deities reside in the human breast."
(William Blake 'The Proverbs of Hell')

"Magic is the first and last religion of the world ... We're joined to everything that was, is and will be. From one end of the Imajica to the other."

The Imajica consists of four Reconciled Dominions and a Fifth, our Earth, separated from the others by the In Ovo, an etheric phantom zone where protean things, both innocent and lethal, are imprisoned.

Five is the number of man and existence; the essence of being, mental inspiration and intellectual synthesis. It represents the centre of the manifest universe, the four elements brought together by the essential fifth to form the undivided Self.

Art forger John Furie Zacharias (also known as Gentle) is one of the Maestros whose role it is to Reconcile Earth with the rest of the Imajica.

Two hundred years previously an attempt at a Reconciliation failed horribly. Gentle (who was then known as Sartori) bound the Mystif Pie'oh'pah to place him under a spell of forgetfulness; and Gentle's former supporters formed a society, the Tabula Rasa, for the repression of all magic.

The members of the Tabula Rasa vowed to keep magic out of the Fifth Dominion, and to prevent another attempt at a Reconciliation; but for the sake of all the souls in Limbo, the Reconciliation must go ahead once the Maestro has remembered himself.

Gentle can remember no further back than a decade. He buries himself in one love affair after another in the hope that one of his "living mirrors" will find in him "some undiscovered self". He fools himself into thinking that if he finds the perfect woman he will find the inner peace he craves, yet not realising the love he seeks is neither a woman nor a man, but the androgyne Pie'oh'pah. Thus each affair ends in near tragedy and Gentle's emptiness remains.

A chance meeting with Pie'oh'pah stirs something in Gentle, and the two of them begin a journey across the Reconciled Dominions that brings Gentle face to face with God.

Imajica is a book of revelations that deals in part with the coming of the millennium. Gods die and men become immortal; cities fall and are born anew from the waters of a flood, and the singleminded Piscean God, Hapexamendios, makes way for the repressed Aquarian Goddesses to return to power within the Imajica.

It is a classic Hero's Journey that brings Gentle into contact with many Archetypes: Judith Odell as Anima, Lover, Everywoman; Sartori as Brother and Shadow, Pie'oh'pah the Androgyne symbol of union of opposites, and Gentle himself as Magus, Lover and Trickster (in his role as faker of art).

Gentle, like *Cabal*'s Boone and *Weaveworld*'s Cal, is both the undoer and the healer of the Otherworld. They are all trespassers unwittingly causing chaos, which they alone must put right.

Imajica describes the journey of a soul. Man has broken free of his Conscious mind (the isolated Fifth Dominion), successfully negotiated the Unconscious (the In Ovo), and travelled through the Collective Unconscious (the Reconciled Dominions) to discover the God residing in himself.

map of the mind

"I sing the progress of a deathless soul,"
(John Donne)

The Puzzlebox Hell, the Fugue, Midian, Quiddity, the Imajica.

Together, these five worlds make up a map of the mind, and the stories set in these worlds mark the borders of its various lands.

We follow Barker's characters on their journeys through life and beyond death, and share their experiences of the magical inner world, which, in turn enriches us.

In *The Hellbound Heart* literal death frees the soul of the egoist Frank so that it may begin its spiritual journey; just as in life, negative personality traits and outmoded ideals must be 'killed off' so that a new and better Self may emerge.

The story of *Weaveworld* stresses the importance of the Unconscious. When Cal is denied access to the Fugue (the Unconscious) he falls rapidly into a decline. It is only when he is able to unite Conscious and Unconscious, by allowing the Fugue to exist in the mundane world, that he is able to function properly as a human being. The dreamworld of the Unconscious is important in everyone's life, and to repress or ignore it is not conducive to a healthy mind and body.

Cabal's Boone makes the trip down into the Unconscious (the underground city of Midian) where he discovers the beast within, and by learning to embrace it, comes to terms with his own duality, and finds the inner peace he has long craved.

The Great and Secret Show concerns the dream sea, Quiddity, and a battle between four shamans, two of whom want to control it, and two who want to protect it. Quiddity is the collective Unconscious: the source of dreams, art, religion; everything that is creative and magical about the human mind. The wisdom of the Collective Unconscious is vital for the spiritual growth of mankind. This pool of knowledge belongs to everyone, collectively and individually. But its usefulness is in the fact that it is unconscious; that it can impart its wisdom in the form of dreams and flashes of inspiration. The human mind is not yet evolved enough to handle the world of the Collective Unconscious on a conscious level. Therefore, for the time being at least, it must remain the stuff of dreams.

Finally we turn to *Imajica*. Not only does this story represent the final stage of the individuation process by allowing the hero to discover the God within, the Higher Self; it also describes a complete soul journey, encompassing all the elements of the previous four stories. The isolated Fifth Dominion represents the conscious mind, and leaving it signifies the beginning of the soul journey. The In Ovo, with its dark protean creatures is the Unconscious, a place where our darker aspects dwell. The lands of the Reconciled Dominions form the Collective Unconscious where magic abounds, but is not accessible from the conscious world of the Fifth Dominion; and the Holy City of Hapexamendios is the home of the Higher Self.

The process of individuation is an ongoing one. The human spirit is constantly growing throughout our lives. All experience causes changes in consciousness, but the greatest and most beneficial changes are caused by that which is experienced at a subconscious level.

One of the most direct forms of this kind of experience, is gained through the arts, particularly through fantastic fiction, where we allow ourselves, quite literally, to enter other worlds and experience very different lifestyles through the eyes of its peoples.

part two

sleeping with the anima

66 I want
to stir up
the Jungian
mud,
enter the
symbollic life
that we all
live between
our ears.
99

CLIVE BARKER
1987

sleeping with
the anima

To find realistic female characters created by a male writer is rare in any genre; rarer still in the genres of Horror and Fantasy where images of women as victims and sex-toys persist. Clive Barker's work is an oasis in a desert of stereotypes. His women are stripped bare of superficial glamour, and are beautiful in the way only real women can be beautiful.

He succeeds where others fail in remembering that women are people first, multi-faceted and many-hued. His women cannot be categorised as Madonnas or whores; housewives or harridans; they are all these things and more.

These women are easily identified with, and their higher qualities ones which we can aspire to own. They are friends, sisters, selves, each with the archetypal element that enables them to hit the spot.

Every one of Barker's women is different, yet they share the common bonds of individuality and strength of character. They have their fears and failings, as do all people; they are as capable of indifference as they are passion; and while their sweet faces may drive their beholders to distraction, to paraphrase the shaman Tesla, they know how to enjoy a good fart.

In almost every story, the women are the ones with the power. They may at first appear uncertain of this power or even of themselves, but by the end of the story they are transformed, and their transformation sits well on them. All are powerful examples of female archetypes, and are fitting choices to people the new myths of the coming Aquarian Age; as they are each a Goddess in Her most diverse incarnation.

To begin to explore this aspect of Barker's fiction, we turn first to a woman whose power manifests itself in a very physical way ...

JACQUELINE ESS

HER WILL AND TESTAMENT

This story from the *Books of Blood* features a woman with the power to alter flesh in accordance with her will. Jacqueline is unaware of the latent power that will eventually turn her into a mythic figure. She first unleashes it on the patronising doctor to whom her husband sends her after her failed suicide attempt:

"Women have certain needs ..." he tells her.

But what could he know of women's needs? He's not a woman. Be a woman, Jacqueline thinks.

In answer to her unspoken command, the doctor's body begins to change. His chest swells into a semblance of a bosom, ripping open as it does so. His hips widen and fracture, spilling his bowels onto the floor.

Jacqueline is at first repulsed by what she has done, but that doesn't stop her going to work on her adulterous husband, making him literally "shut up".

His body collapses in on itself, flesh and bone grinding down to occupy "a smaller and yet smaller space".

"... As she came out of her ecstasy she saw Ben sitting on the floor, shut up into a space about the size of one of his fine leather suitcases, while blood, bile and lymphatic fluid pulsed weakly from his hushed body.

My God, she thought, this can't be my husband. He's never been as tidy as that."

Despite her formidable power, there is a man who sees her uniqueness and loves her for it. He is Oliver Vassi, an old lawyer friend of her late husband's. Vassi describes her as beautiful, though not in any conventional sense:

"Her face was plainly that of a woman in her early forties ... But she had a power to transform herself ... making that face as various as the sky."

One night, Vassi watches Jacqueline sleeping, and catches a glimpse of her remarkable powers, as her flesh reconfigures in response to her dreams:

"Her lips bloomed from her bone, boiling up into a slavering tower of skin; her hair swirled around her head ... her cheeks formed furrows and ridges like the ritual scars on a warrior ..."

Jacqueline leaves Vassi in search of someone who can teach her to use her power. Her first choice, Titus Pettifer, supposedly the most influential man in the country, turns out to be ineffectual, and hardly in a position to teach Jacqueline about power. He is eventually dealt with in her own peculiar way, and she moves on once more.

Eventually, the gift that could have made Jacqueline so powerful reduces her to a prostitute. She spends all her time chained to a mattress to prevent her from destroying herself, watched over by Koos, her pimp.

Vassi, who has been searching for Jacqueline ever since she left, traces her to Amsterdam. In search of solace in the red-light district Vassi is approached by Koos who offers to take him to Jacqueline's room but warns him he will not survive one night with her. The price for access to her shrine is high: the shirt off his back, his jewellery, in short, everything he owns. Vassi pays willingly.

So at last he and Jacqueline are together:

"My God, she thought, we are together.

"And thinking they were together, her will was made flesh. Under his lips her features dissolved, becoming the red sea he'd dreamed of ... common waters made of thought and bone. ... Tangled in a wash of love they thought themselves extinguished, and were."

Jacqueline Ess typifies the woman trapped by her own power; a power she cannot control and which, inevitably, can only destroy her. It is a mark of her humanity that Jacqueline rejects the temptation to re-make herself as a Goddess and chooses instead to die with the only man who truly loves her.

JULIA

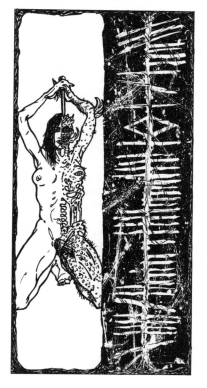

THE HELLBOUND HEART

"No poison's half so bad as Julia."
(*John Donne 'Julia'*)

Beneath the facade of the "perfect hausfrau" beats the heart of a demon.

After a bout of joyless sex with Frank, her future brother-in-law, Julia falls head first into obsession. As the years pass, with no word from Frank, the memory of their coupling is transformed into a momentous event. Julia grows to despise her lacklustre husband Rory and dreams of one day being with reunited with Frank.

Their reunion comes somewhat unexpectedly when she and Rory move into the house where Frank's spirit is imprisoned. When Rory accidentally cuts himself, spilling blood onto the floor, Frank's ghost begins to grow flesh.

After a dull dinner party, Julia decides to retire early. On her way to bed she looks in on the "damp room", as they call the room with the uncomfortable atmosphere. She hears a sound like "a cockroach running behind the skirting boards".

"I hear you" she says, uncertain of whom she is addressing, or even why she has spoken. She moves towards the tapping wall as if summoned. There is light — "a cold luminescence", and segments of the wall begin to shift.

The wall stops moving and something appears that is "ragged enough to be a shadow but too substantial". It is Frank, and he is hideously transformed: "a thing that had been ripped apart and sewn together again with most of its pieces missing or twisted and blackened as if in a furnace".

Julia is not afraid, the creature is far weaker than her, she pities its condition. Frank tells her he needs more blood if he is to survive, and perhaps escape. She remembers him as he used to be, "his roughness ... his insistence" and agrees to supply anything he needs.

Julia "the sweet, the beautiful" picks up a stranger in a bar and takes him back to the house where she plunges a knife into him "... slicing his belly with the ease of a blade in over-ripe cheese".

While she is still in the process of concealing the victim's remains, Rory returns home calling for his sweetheart.

"Sweetheart? she could have laughed but for the terror – she was here if he wanted her – his sweetheart, his honeybun – with ... a dead man in her arms".

Julia finds the killing gets easier with practise. Her second victim is a man whom she first dismisses as being "too big, too confident" until he takes hold of her wrist with "a grip so tight she almost cried out. That was when she knew she was going to have to kill him".

With each progressive feed Frank grows stronger. Julia looks at his pulsing body with no little pride:

"She had made this man, or remade him ... the thrill she felt ... was the thrill of ownership". She imagines that for her efforts Frank will become her grateful pet, that "with time she would have love from this hateful thing, or know the reason why".

But death and rebirth hasn't changed Frank, he is only using her for his own survival, and despite her dreams, Julia realises her obsession will destroy her, and that she lost her grip some time ago "lying on a bed of wedding lace, while Frank beset her neck with kisses."

Julia's fate, after she dies on the blade of Frank's knife, is left to the inventive denizens of Hell, the Cenobites.

Both Julia and Frank are imprisoned: Frank by his selfish desires and Julia by the obsession she mistakes for love. They are alike in many respects, each doomed to live in a hell of their own making, but for Julia she has simply stepped from one hell into another as her oppressively boring life with Rory gives way first to the hell of deception and murder and finally the hell of a living death.

SISTERS IN SORROW

IMMACOLATA AND SUZANNA

"She was beautiful ... her skin gleamed as if oiled ... her mouth was too sculpted; and her eyes – umber one moment, gold the next – too eloquent for the feelings there to be disguised"

Immacolata, a dark descendant of Lilith is, with her two wraith sisters, the Magdalene (a succubus) and the Hag; a perfect example of the triple Lunar Goddess. The three phases of the Moon – waxing, full and waning are personified in mythology by the virgin, the mother and the crone, who are represented in *Weaveworld* by Immacolata, the Magdalene and the Hag.

Immacolata is a paradox. She dresses in a manner that is both "chaste ... and eroticised", a rich sensuality informs her features yet she is a dedicated virgin to whom physical contact is an anathema; and "beneath the incandescent beauty" of a face "as blank as a dead child's" are feelings and thoughts "that would blister the air if given vent".

Exiled to live in the human Kingdom where she is revered and reviled by turns, Immacolata takes refuge in madness as an escape from the banality of the human world. She is discovered by the salesman Shadwell who deciphers the miraculous truths behind her ramblings.

Fuelled by her hatred of the Seerkind who banished her, Immacolata pursues the Fugue down the years with Shadwell as her sidekick. Their plan is to auction the carpet and sell the four great families of the Seerkind into slavery.

The allegiance between Immacolata and the human Shadwell falls apart when Shadwell's ambition to sell the Fugue becomes an ambition to rule it.

At the beginning of the story Immacolata is immensely powerful, even Shadwell fears her as much as he desires her. She seems cold, unknowable and without redeeming features. As her character develops, and humiliation weakens her, she gradually gains our sympathies.

As Immacolata falls, so her 'sister in sorrow' Suzanna Parrish rises.

Of all the story's characters, Suzanna undergoes the most dramatic changes. She first appears as an ordinary human woman on her way to visit Mimi Laschenski, the grandmother she hasn't seen since childhood.

Mimi is the last surviving custodian of the Fugue and now, old and infirm, needs to pass the duty onto Suzanna. The stroke which disabled Mimi has left her unable to speak, and so the best she can do by way of explanation is to give her granddaughter a vision of the carpet. Suzanna is then left to unravel the mystery for herself.

A confrontation with Immacolata turns Suzanna's life on its head. Immacolata unleashes the menstruum, "that stream of bright darkness... an etheric solution in which it was said the wielder could dissolve all experience, and make it again in the image of her desire", and instead of cowering, Suzanna stands in its path and reaches out to catch its light.

"It was like plunging her arm into a torrent of ice cold water ... in which innumerable fish were swimming".

The menstruum, recognising its own, floods Suzanna's body, flowing with the Seerkind blood she inherited from Mimi and waking her dormant powers.

As the story progresses Suzanna becomes more and more powerful. All the decisions are hers: she is the waker and remaker of worlds. Much of that strength is inherited from Mimi, a woman so fiercely protective in her role of custodian she manages to cling onto life long enough to impart vital information to her granddaughter.

Suzanna becomes the Fugue's custodian, a task made more difficult by the fact that she is pursued by Inspector Hobart who believes Suzanna to be a terrorist, and himself to be infused with divine right.

The battle between Suzanna and Hobart is one of constant role reversal, both parties alternately playing the parts of hunter and prey, yet each remaining the antithesis of the other.

Suzanna and Immacolata are more alike than they are different. Although Immacolata, like the Moon, is waning, and Suzanna's power is waxing, the lives of both women are touched by tragedy. Immacolata courts misery, and is, by nature, a tragic figure; the joys of Suzanna's achievements and discoveries are soured by her losses.

They have both been touched by a power that isolates its owner; those who do not possess or understand the menstruum fear its potency, thereby making it its owner's sole comforter. Suzanna's own observation could not be more appropriate: "I'm married to myself".

THE ESSENTIAL
SHAMAN

TESLA
BOMBECK

Screenwriter Tesla Bombeck, the "wild woman of West Hollywood", appears in *The Great and Secret Show* initially as a voice on the other end of a telephone conversation in which she dishes the dirt on comedian Buddy Vance to a journalist who is covering a story about the comedian.

With the benefit of hindsight, we can see that Tesla is destined for greatness. Her first appearance as a disembodied voice seems inauspicious, yet like Voodoo priests, it is part of a shaman's power to be knowledgeable in the private lives of their parishioners; and Tesla boasts a wealth of inside information on the inhabitants of Hollywood.

Three of the basic requirements for a shaman are dual or bi-sexuality; death and resurrection; and acquisition of a guardian animal spirit. By her dress sense alone, Tesla demonstrates the first of her shamanic qualities; to quote the lady herself:

"... most of these shamans ... were a little off in some way. Cross-dressers; gender-fuckers. All things to all men."

And Tesla is certainly that, wearing a man's shirt, women's shoes and unisex trousers lends her ambiguous sexuality. A Mexican bola with the "image of the Madonna" gives her an affinity with the Goddess, as do her earrings, silver being the metal of the Moon, the planet sacred to the Goddess; and the snake design of her jewellery gives her occult power, as snakes are symbolic of both the Occult and of healing.

Tesla is thrust into the main frame of the action when the shaman

Fletcher notices a stigmata-like wound in the palm of her hand and realises that she is the one who must take over from him and protect the dream sea Quiddity.

Fletcher tells her she must first go to his abandoned laboratory in a disused Jesuit Mission, and destroy his "great work"; the evolution spurring solution, the nuncio. Tesla drives to the Mission where she meets Raul, once an ape, now transformed by the nuncio into a man.

While Tesla is at the Mission, she meets the second shamanic requirement of death and resurrection when she is shot and has to recreate her body through the power of her imagination.

As she lays injured and rapidly losing consciousness, the shaman Kissoon pulls her into the time loop which imprisons him. She is drawn out of herself and her mind is whisked away over the desert of New Mexico, to a white painted hut. Tesla enters the hut and finds Kissoon sitting by a small fire in the middle of the floor.

Kissoon asks Tesla to close the door behind her, but she cannot do this as only her spirit is here, her body is back at the mission.

"Just imagine yourself." Kissoon tells her.

"She thought hard of the body she'd grown into over a period of thirty-two years. It was by no means perfect, but at least it was all hers. No silicone; no nips and tucks ... most of all she liked her face, with its quirks and laugh-lines ... to imagine was the trick ... she remembered her face smiling back at her when she stepped from the shower in the morning. It was a fine feeling, maturing in that flesh,"

Kissoon wants to use Tesla's body as a vehicle in which to escape from the time loop.

Tesla becomes suspicious of Kissoon's motives when she glimpses him "transfigured ... his upper body covered in blood... he knew she saw, because his hands went up to cover the stains, but his hands and arms were also running with blood. Was it his? Before she could look to find a wound he had control of the vision once again."

With his grip on her released, Tesla is dragged back the way she came to the Mission where Raul is waiting. He tells her that for a time her body actually vanished "'First like fog,' he said 'Then ... just gone.'".

It is then that Tesla notices her body is the wrong way round; she has imagined herself the way she is most used to seeing: as a reflection in a mirror.

"Reversed and resurrected", Tesla is now ready to protect Quiddity from its would-be controllers, and to close the schism, opened by one such trespasser, which threatens to allow the Iad Uroboros (the nightmare creatures who live on the other side of Quiddity) to enter the waking world.

While Tesla is busy with her new mission, Kissoon tricks Raul into vacating his body, which is destroyed when Kissoon is ultimately defeated.

Tesla discovers Raul's terrified spirit trapped in Kissoon's loop. She cannot leave her friend in this state, so despite her initial reservations, she allows the spirit of Raul to enter her body.

With this act, Tesla achieves the third shamanic requirement, and becomes a trinity of Woman, Man and Ape: Anima, Animus, Animal.

It is now apparent that Tesla is the long awaited saviour whom psychics say is "sometimes ... a man, sometimes a woman. Sometimes not even human."

Of all Barker's women Tesla undergoes perhaps the greatest transformation, yet everything that happens to her is taken very much in her stride. She calls herself a non-believer, pours scorn on each and every religion, but she is open to having those opinions challenged, and is more than willing to learn about and understand life's great mysteries.

By the end of *The Great and Secret Show* Tesla's mission has only just begun. She is aware that the Iad Uroboros will try to enter our world again, and is busy gathering a team to help her prevent an invasion.

Despite the vastness of the task ahead of her, Tesla is the equal of it. Her role is one she was born to play. From the moment Fletcher noticed the wound in her palm, Tesla's idea of herself began to change. She remarks to journalist Nathan Grillo:

"I can do this, Grillo, I'm weird enough ... all things to all men ... I want to be that."

With her absorption of Raul's spirit Tesla realises that dream, and becomes a truer shaman than Fletcher, the Jaff (Fletcher's evil counterpart) or Kissoon could ever hope to be.

Whereas most shamans experiences of death and resurrection, dual or bisexuality and communion with an animal guide are symbolic, Tesla's are literal, making her the essential shaman.

THE ETERNAL WOMAN

JUDITH ODELL

"Yet but of Judith no such book
as she"
(John Donne 'To the Lady Bedford')

"Not once so far had they mentioned her by name ... She was she, her, the woman; an absolute and invisible power. Her men seemed to have their feet on solid ground, but in truth they drifted like the kites, tethered to reality only by the memory of her."

"The woman" in *Imajica* is Judith Odell, the perfect beauty, the archetypal poet's Muse, the Eternal Woman. Her estranged husband Charlie Estabrook thinks of her as:

"like some fugitive from some more perfect place. Her skin was flawless ... her body was long, like her hair, like her fingers ... her eyes ... had every season of every leaf in them: the twin greens of spring and high summer, the golds of autumn, and, in her rages, black midwinter rot."

So obsessed is Estabrook, that when Judith leaves him, he hires someone to kill her. The assassin is the mystif Pie'oh'pah.

Pie tracks Judith to New York where she is Christmas shopping. Judith is in the menswear department of Bloomingdales when she thinks she sees Gentle, a former lover. She dives through the crowds after him but when she finally catches up with him she finds it is not Gentle at all but a stranger.

"This black man, his ringleted hair gleaming on his shoulders, was not Gentl e... her eyes lingered on the stranger's face, and for a heartbeat, or less, his features blurred, and in their flux ... she saw Gentle ... the stranger turned, Gentle was gone."

As she walks back to the apartment where she is staying, she remembers her affair with Gentle, over some six years ago, that began with a recurring dream.

"The scenario was always the same. She was lying naked on bare boards in an empty room, not bound but somehow bounded and a man whose face she could never see, his mouth so sweet it was like eating candy to kiss him, made violent love to her. Only this time the fire that burned in the grate close by showed her the face of the dream-lover, and it had been Gentle's face."

The 'dream' is not a dream, however, but a memory.

Like Pygmalion's living statue, this Judith was not born, but created by the Maestro Sartori, an ageless, everlasting and more perfect copy of the original Judith.

Yet despite this, never does she appear to be anything but a real, fully functioning human being. We experience much of the story through her eyes, and indeed, share her surprise when she finds she has a double in the Reconciled Dominions of the Imajica. The Judith copy, our Judith, is so well crafted a character, she is the true Judith, and the original has become the 'other'.

That she came into being through magical means makes her a thing of magic herself. When she takes a small blue stone from her estranged husband's collection of Imajical things, she embarks on a spiritual journey where she floats out of the window of her flat, and through the rainsoaked streets, to witness fragments of other women's lives:

"... slivers of dramas she could only guess at. A woman in an upper room, staring down at a dress laid on a stripped bed; another at a window, tears falling from beneath her closed lids as she swayed to music Jude couldn't hear ... None of them women she knew, but all quite familiar ... she'd felt like all of them at some time or other: forsaken; powerless; yearning."

Judith witnesses nine such scenes before coming to the one that is the reason for her journey. She is taken to a cellar whose walls are lined with books. Her gaze is drawn to the wall behind the shelves which has the same blue tint as the stone. She passes through the wall where she finds the bound cocooned body of a woman. Her spirit enters the dead woman and wakes her, whereupon Judith's mission is at an end, and she returns to her room and her own body.

Apart from the primary purpose of her journey, which is to wake the bound woman, Judith's flight also serves to illustrate that she is the embodiment of all that women are, she is the Archetypal female: Madonna, whore, frail beauty, strident amazon. Judith completely transcends her condition of being a kind of 'homunculus' and even goes on to become a mother, thus confirming to herself that she is real in her own right, and no longer a 'mere' copy of the other Judith.

the awakening
woman

The age of Aquarius is a Goddess Age, and the mythology should reflect this with strong female characters.

These six of Barker's female characters are powerfully original creations whose archetypal elements give them a mythic quality.

Jacqueline Ess is a vengeful Kali whose kindest gift is death. She brings death to her victims and to the man she loves, all of whom suffer as much without her as with her.

Julia, whose obsession carries her off to Hell, becomes a vampire by proxy when she kills for blood to revive her beloved Frank. Like a Dark Goddess, she takes the blood of her disciples (men who can't believe their luck when the beautiful Julia picks them up in bars) and is totally without mercy. Even her love for the skinless Frank is on the grounds that she revived him, clothed his bones with the blood of her 'worshippers', and therefore owns him.

Immacolata and Suzanna are two sides of the same coin. Both women possess a power that can be used to heal or harm, and both make very different choices as to how they will use that power.

The shaman Tesla is a mind healer, a dream warrior and the saviour who will lead us into the new Millennium. Her power is that of the imagination, the collective unconscious. Only a shaman such as Tesla can wield this power successfully because she is "all things to all men": a trinity of woman, man, ape; mother, son and animal ghost in one body. Tesla is the perfect embodiment of the Aquarian ethos of thought made solid and dreams made flesh.

Just as the worlds of the *Imajica* represent the different components of the psyche, so Judith represents the many aspects of the feminine. Her spiritual journey instigated by the blue stone shows that Judith is Woman in her every guise. Muse, Mistress, Wife, Mother; at some stage in her life Judith is each and all of them.

Perhaps in many years, these characters will have passed into the folk tales of the future. Perhaps Immacolata will be mentioned in the same breath as other fairy tale sorceresses; and instead of the Sandman, perhaps the shaman Tesla will be the bringer of dreams.

But that future is a long way off. What is important is that we have these stories now; that we are reading these myths, and understanding them as they are being created instead of with hindsight.

A DREAM WHOSE SHAPES RETURN

" 'People know stuff... without realising it, they know.

That's what makes us wonderful.' "

THE GREAT AND SECRET SHOW

There are dreams that end and are forgotten as soon as we wake and there are dreams that continue beyond sleep, their themes expanding, their characters taking on new depths. Just as there are dreams and dreams, so there are stories and stories.

Imagine a story through which runs a second story, like a fine invisible thread, that can neither be seen nor grasped in a physical sense, but which attaches itself to some unknown part of us.

These are the stories of Clive Barker. Beneath the fiction lies a truth that is perceived at a deeper level: the truth of fable, of fairytale and of myth.

Every story works on different levels. On one level they are each an adventure; classic heroes' tales of love, death and madness; on another they stage a sensual and emotional assault, dragging us out of our everyday lives into a world of wonders and terrors.

Beyond that lies the unwritten story, the invisible thread that winds through the labyrinth of the dream pool, rounding up the creatures and shapes that cause us to react in ways we cannot explain, that awaken the buried memories we carry in every cell.

Barker's stories take place in a "time out of time"; the settings are contemporary, the people very much of the modern age, yet the themes and the characters themselves are timeless, enabling the stories to remain as relevant in future years as they are today. Faeryland in a carpet; Hell in a puzzlebox: shapes that will return long after the age that spawned them has passed. Because nothing ever begins. Before the art, the dream; before the dream, the archetype; and before that the Collective Unconscious; the soup from which comes everything: dreams, art, archetype and myth.

With this skill of sieving the waters of the Collective Unconscious, Barker takes things that seem unimaginable and makes us believe. His intuitive grasp of the things we know yet don't know makes his work important. A new mythology for a new Age.

"After tonight there would be only one world, to live in and to dream ... There was time for all miracles now. For ghosts and transformations; for passion and ambiguity; for noon-day visions and midnight glory. Time in abundance. For nothing ever begins. And this story, having no beginning, will have no end."
(*Weaveworld*)

CLIVE
BARKER

Past,
Present,
Future

" It's just
my dream
to be
known as
an imaginer,
as someone
who makes
worlds.
"

CLIVE BARKER

clive barker biography

Clive Barker, born in Liverpool on October 5th 1952, is a Libran, and by the Chinese horoscope system, a Water Dragon.

At the age of nineteen, Barker made a low-budget black and white film, 'Salome', shot on 8mm. In 1975, he made a second film, 'The Forbidden', based on the Faust legend, shot entirely in negative, and starring Peter Atkins.

After leaving university, Barker toured Europe and the United Kingdom with his theatre group the Dog Company, staging original Grand Guignol-style productions such as, 'The Magician'; 'The History of the Devil'; 'Frankenstein in Love' and 'Subtle Bodies'.

His short story collections, *The Books of Blood*, were written for the entertainment of his friends and not originally intended for publication. However, the stories went on to become hugely successful, provoking the now legendary quote from best-selling Horror writer Stephen King, "I have seen the future of Horror. His name is Clive Barker." and firmly establishing Barker as one of the most original and daring exponents of Horror and Dark Fantasy.

In 1985, between volumes one to three, and volumes four to six of *The Books of Blood* came Barker's first novel, *The Damnation Game*, a cyclical Faustian tale in which Marty, a gambler and ex-convict is hired as a bodyguard by millionaire Joseph Whitehead, a former gambler and thief, who owes his empire to the powerful Last European, Mamoulian who sacrificed his own soul in return for his terrifying powers.

After seeing of two of his screenplays, *Rawhead Rex* and *Underworld* turned into disappointing films Barker went on to direct his own feature film. The film, made with a modest budget and shot largely in a house in North London, was *Hellraiser*. Based on his novella *The Hellbound Heart*, *Hellraiser* became a landmark in the history of genre films with its uncompromising stance of 'showing the monster', and going a long way to disprove the clichÈ that what is implied is more frightening than what is shown.

Barker's next film *Nightbreed*, based on the novel *Cabal* took the idea of showing the monster a stage further: the so-called monsters, the Breed, are the heroes, and the actual monsters are the humans who hound them for the crime of being different.

Barker's novel *Weaveworld*, described by J G Ballard as coming from "a powerful and fascinating writer with a brilliant imagination." marked a move away from Horror towards the kind of Dark Fantasy he is associated with today.

After *Weaveworld*, came *The Great and Secret Show*. Kirkus called it, "one of the most powerful overtly metaphysical novels of recent years." The New York Times described it as "a cross between 'Gravity's Rainbow' and Tolkien's 'Lord of the Rings'."

1991 saw the publication of *Imajica*, Barker's biggest book to date, both in size (hardback edition 854 pages) and in subject matter. *Imajica*, truly a book of Revelations, deals with the death of God and the re-establishment of magic as "the first and last religion of the world".

In 1992 Clive Barker gave us *The Thief of Always*, a totally new children's fable which is soon to be made into an animated feature film by Paramount Studios.

As if writing and film-making wasn't enough Clive Barker is also a talented artist whose work has been exhibited in New York's Bess Cutler Gallery.

bibliography

CLIVE BARKER'S BOOKS OF BLOOD, VOLUME ONE. (1984)
Introduction by Ramsey Campbell; The Book of Blood; The Midnight Meat Train; The Yattering and Jack; Pig Blood Blues; Sex, Death and Starshine; In the Hills, The Cities.

CLIVE BARKER'S BOOKS OF BLOOD, VOLUME TWO (1984)
Dread; Hell's Event; Jacqueline Ess: Her Will and Testament; The Skins of the Fathers; New Murders in the Rue Morgue

CLIVE BARKER'S BOOKS OF BLOOD, VOLUME THREE (1984)
Son of Celluloid; Rawhead Rex; Confessions of a (Pornographer's) Shroud; Scapegoats; Human Remains.

THE DAMNATION GAME (1985)

CLIVE BARKER'S BOOKS OF BLOOD, VOLUME FOUR (1985)
The Body Politic; The Inhuman Condition; Revelations; Down, Satan!; The Age of Desire.

CLIVE BARKER'S BOOKS OF BLOOD, VOLUME FIVE (1985)
The Forbidden; The Madonna; Babel's Children; In the Flesh.

CLIVE BARKER'S BOOKS OF BLOOD, VOLUME SIX (1985)
The Life of Death; How Spoilers Bleed; Twilight at the Towers; The Last Illusion; The Book of Blood (A Postscript): On Jerusalem Street.

WEAVEWORLD (1987)

THE HELLBOUND HEART (1987)

CABAL (1988)

THE GREAT AND SECRET SHOW (1989)

IMAJICA (1991)

THE THIEF OF ALWAYS (1992)

EVERVILLE (1994)

It was not music that finally picked her up, nor the hands of the invisible throng. It was a shout, which rose above the trumpet echoes, and filled her with alarm...

EVERVILLE

Everville is the second book of the Art and is a sequel to The Great and Secret Show. It is published by HarperCollins on 29 September 1994.

The following pages contain an excerpt from chapter three.

"Five years ago, in his bestseller The Great and Secret Show, Clive Barker mesmerised millions of readers worldwide with an extraordinary vision of human passions and possibilities.

Welcome to a new volume in that epic adventure. Welcome to Everville."

It was not music that finally picked her up, nor the hands of the invisible throng. It was a shout, which rose above the trumpet echoes, and filled her with alarm.

'Damn you, O'Connell!' She knew the voice. It was Whitney. 'God in Heaven! What have you done?' he yelled.

She got to her feet and started towards his din. Her eyes were not yet accustomed to the gloom after the brightness of the blizzard, and the further from the edge of the forest she ventured, the darker it became, but the rage in Whitney's voice spurred her on, careless of what lay in her path. The trumpets had fallen silent. Perhaps the angels had heard his rants, she thought, and would not float their harmonies on tainted air; or perhaps they were simply watching to see what human rage was like.

'You knew!' Whitney was yelling. 'You brought us into Hell!'

Maeve could see him now, moving between the trees, calling after his quarry into the shadows.

'O'Connell? O'Connell! You'll burn in a lake of fire for this. Burn and burn and -'

He stopped; swung round, his eyes finding Maeve with terrible speed. Before she could retreat, he yelled: 'I see you! Come out, you little bitch!'

Maeve had no choice. He had her in the sights of his rifle. And now, as she approached hum between the trees, she saw that he was not alone. Sheldon, Sturgis and Pottruck were just a few yards from him. Sturgis was crouched against a tree, terrified of something in the branches above him, where his rifle was pointed. Pottruck was watching Whitney's antics with a bemused expression on his oafish face.

'O'Connell?' Whitney yelled. 'I got your little girl here.' He adjusted his aim, squinted for accuracy. 'I got her right between the eyes if I pull the trigger. An' I'm going to do it. Hear me, O'Connell?'

'Don't shoot,' Sturgis said. 'You'll bring it back.'

'It'll come anyway,' Whitney said. 'O'Connell sent it to fetch our souls.'

'Oh Jesus Christ in Heaven ...' Sturgis sobbed.

'Stand right there,' Whitney said to Maeve. 'And you call to your Daddy and you tell him to keep his demon away from us or I'll kill you.'

'He hasn't ... hasn't got any demons,' Maeve said. She didn't want Whitney to know that she was afraid, but she couldn't help herself. Tears came anyway.

'You just tell him,' Whitney said, 'you just call.' He pushed the rifle in Maeve's direction, so that it was a foot from her face. 'If you don't I'll kill you. You're the Devil's child's what you are. Ain't no crime killing muck like you. Go on. Call him.'

'Papa?'

'Louder!'

'Papa?'

There was no reply from the shadows. 'He doesn't hear me.'

'I hear you child,' said her father. She looked towards the voice and there he was, coming towards her out of the murk.

'Drop your rifle!' Pottruck yelled to him.

Even as he did, the trumpets began again, louder than ever. The music clutched at Maeve's heart with such force she started to gasp for breath.

'What's wrong?' she heard her father say, and glanced back in his direction to see him start towards her.

'Stay where you are!' Whitney yelled, but her father kept running.

There was no second warning. Whitney simply fired, not once but twice. One bullet struck him in the shoulder, the other in the stomach. He stumbled on towards her, but before he could take two strides, his legs gave out beneath him, and he fell down.

'Papa!' she yelled, and would have gone to him, but then the trumpets began another volley, and as their music rose up in her, bursts of white light blotted out the world, and she dropped to the ground in a swoon.

'I hear it coming ...'

'Shut up, Sturgis.'

'It is! It's coming again. Whitney! What do we do?'

Sturgis' shrill shouts pricked Maeve awake. She opened her eyes to see her father lying where he had fallen. He was still moving, she saw, his hands clutching rhythmically at his belly, his legs twitching.

'Whitney!' Sturgis was screaming. 'It's coming back.'

She could not see him from where she lay, but she could hear the thrashing of the branches, as though the wind had suddenly risen. Whitney was praying.

'Our Lord, who art in Heaven ...'

Maeve moved her head a little, in the hope of glimpsing the trio without drawing attention to herself. Whitney was on his knees, Sturgis was cowering against the tree, and Pottruck was staring up into the canopy waving wildly: 'Come on, you fucking shit! Come on!'

Certain that she was forgotten, Maeve got to her feet cautiously, reaching out to grab hold of the nearest tree trunk for support. She looked back to her father, who had raised his head a couple of inches off the ground and was staring at Pottruck as he fired up into the thrashing branches.

Sturgis yelled, 'Christ, no!', Whitney started to rise from his kneel, and in that same moment, a form that Maeve's bewildered eyes could not quite distinguish from the branches – it had their sweep and their darkness – swooped upon Pottruck.

Whatever it was, it was no angel. There were no features here. There was no gold or scarlet or blue. The beast was naked, of that she was reasonably certain, and its flesh gleamed. That was all she had time to grasp before it picked Pottruck up and carried him off, up into the canopy.

He screamed and screamed, and Maeve, though she hated the man with a passion, wished he might be saved from his torment, if only to stop his din. She covered her ears but his cries found their way between her fingers, mounting in volume as a terrible rain fell from the branches. First came the rifle, then blood, pattering down. Then one of Pottruck's arms, followed by a piece of flesh she could not distinguish; and another. And still he screamed, though the patter of the blood had become a downpour, and the snaking part of his innards dropped from the tree in a glistening loop.

Suddenly, Sturgis was rising from his hiding place, and began to fire into the tree. Perhaps he put Pottruck from his misery, perhaps the beast simply took out the man's throat. Whichever, the terrible sound ceased, and a moment later Pottruck's body, so mangled it looked barely human, fell from the branches and lay steaming on the ground.

The canopy stilled. Sturgis backed away into the shadows, stifling his sobs. Maeve froze, praying that Whitney would go with him. But he did not. Instead he started towards her father.

'See what you did, calling the Evil One?' he said.

'I ... didn't ... call anybody,' Harman gasped.

'You tell it to go back to the pit, O'Connell. You tell it!'

Maeve looked back in Sturgis' direction. The man had fled. But her gaze fell on Pottruck's rifle, which lay beneath the dripping branches a yard from his corpse.

'You repent,' Whitney was saying to Harmon. 'You send that devil back where it came from, or I'm going to blow off your hands, then your pecker, till you're begging to repent.'

With Sturgis gone and Whitney's back turned, Maeve didn't need much caution. Eyes cast up towards the branches, where she was certain the beast still squatted, she started towards the rifle. She could see no sign of the creature – the mesh of branches was too thick – but she could feel its gaze on her.

'Please ...' she whispered to it, the syllables too soft to attract Whitney's attention, '... don't hurt ... me ...'

The BRITISH FANTASY SOCIETY

*T*here is a group of people who know all the latest publishing news and gossip. They enjoy the very best in fiction from some of the hottest new talents around. They can read articles by and about their favourite authors and know in advance when those authors' books are being published. These people belong to the British Fantasy Society.

The BFS publishes a regular Newsletter as well as numerous magazines containing fantasy and horror fiction, speculative articles, artwork, reviews, interviews, comment and much more. They also organise the acclaimed annual FantasyCon convention to which publishers, editors and authors flock to hear the announcement of the coveted British Fantasy Awards, voted on by the members.

Membership of the British Fantasy Society is open to everyone. The annual UK subscription is £15.00 which covers the Newsletter and the magazines. To join, send monies payable to 'The British Fantasy Society', together with your name and address, to:

THE BFS SECRETARY, c/o 2 HARWOOD STREET, STOCKPORT, SK4 1JJ

Overseas membership: £18 Europe, $32 USA and £23 everywhere else in the world.

The BFS reserves the right to raise membership fees. Should the fee change, applicants for membership will be advised.

'I sense that all the roads I walk along
lead to the same country, and that is
the space between my ears.'

CLIVE BARKER

Admired artist, creative film maker, and acclaimed
bestselling author, Clive Barker once again will
mesmerise millions of readers worldwide with his
extraordinary vision of human passions and
possibilities. Enthralling, chilling and charged
with unbridled eroticism.

EVERVILLE